SELECTED CLARINET SOLOS

MW01165346

This classic collection provides the student and teacher a unique sourcebook of compositions chosen for their technique, phrasing, and melodic beauty. Includes the piano accompaniment.

Cover photograph by Randall Wallace

This book Copyright © 1941 (Renewed) by Amsco Music Publishing Company
A Division of Music Sales Corporation, New York

All rights reserved. No part of this book may be
reproduced in any form or by any electronic or mechanical means,
including information storage and retrieval systems,
without permission in writing from the publisher.

Order No. AM 40221
International Standard Book Number: 0.8256.2043.0

Exclusive Distributors:
Music Sales Corporation
257 Park Avenue South, New York, NY 10010 USA
Music Sales Limited
8/9 Frith Street, London W1V 5TZ England
Music Sales Pty. Limited
120 Rothschild Street, Rosebery, Sydney, NSW 2018, Australia

Printed in the United States of America by
Vicks Lithograph and Printing Corporation

AMSCO PUBLICATIONS
NEW YORK/LONDON/SYDNEY

Selected Clarinet Solos

Ballet Music from "Rosamunde"
I. Andante

F. SCHUBERT

Copyright MCMXLI—by Amsco Music Publishing Co.

Ballet Music from "Rosamunde"
II. Andantino

F. SCHUBERT

Copyright MCMXLI—by Amsco Music Publishing Co.

Walter's Prize Song
from "DIE MEISTERSINGER"

R. WAGNER

Copyright MCMXLI—by Amsco Music Publishing Co.

Salut d'amour
(LOVE'S GREETING)

E. ELGAR, Op. 12

Copyright MCMXLI—by Amsco Music Publishing Co.

Serenade Badine

GABRIEL - MARIE

Copyright MCMXLI—by Amsco Music Publishing Co

CODA

CODA

Melodie

P. I. TSCHAIKOWSKY, Op. 42, No. 3

Copyright MCMXLI—by Amsco Music Publishing Co.

To Spring

EDVARD GRIEG, Op. 43, No. 6

Copyright MCMXLI—by Amsco Music Publishing Co.

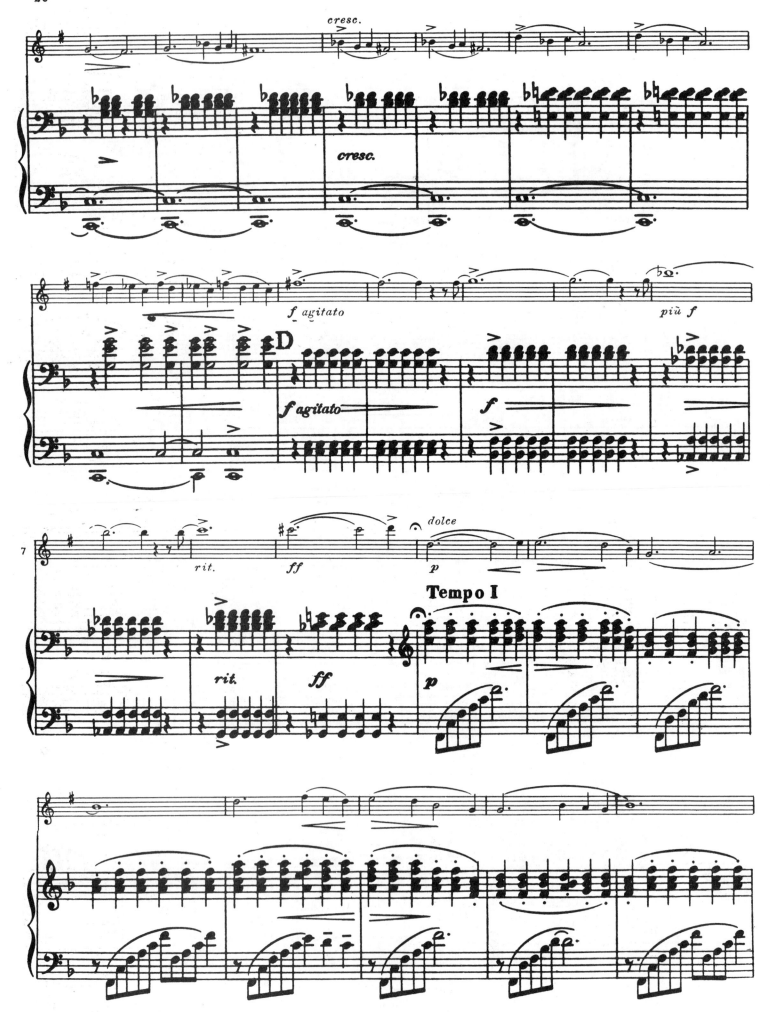

Melodie

MORITZ MOSZKOWSKI, Op. 18, No. 1

Copyright MCMXLI—by Amsco Music Publishing Co.

Au Matin

BENJAMIN GODARD

Copyright MCMXLI by Amsco Music Publishing Co. Inc., N.Y. City

Made in U. S. A.

Intermezzo
from "MIDSUMMER NIGHT'S DREAM"

F. MENDELSSOHN

Copyright MCMXLI by Amsco Music Publishing Co. Inc., N.Y. City

Made in U.S.A.

Nocturne
from "MIDSUMMER NIGHT'S DREAM"

F. MENDELSSOHN

Con moto tranquillo

Con moto tranquillo

Copyright MCMXLI by Amsco Music Publishing Co. Inc., N.Y. City   Made in U. S. A.

My Heart At Thy Sweet Voice
"SAMSON AND DELILAH"

C. SAINT-SAËNS

Copyright MCMXLI by Amsco Music Publishing Co. Inc., N.Y. City

Made in U.S.A.

Poco piu lento

Poco piu lento

Anitra's Dance
(PEER GYNT)

EDWARD GRIEG

Copyright MCMXLI by Amsco Music Publishing Co., Inc., N.Y. City

Made in U. S. A.

Caro Mio Ben

G. GIORDANI

Copyright MCMXLI by Amsco Music Publishing Co. Inc., N.Y. City

Made in U. S. A.

Connais-tu le pays
from "MIGNON"

A. THOMAS

Copyright MCMXLI by Amsco Music Publishing Co. Inc., N.Y. City.

Made in U.S.A

Miserere
from "IL TROVATORE"

G. VERDI

Copyright MCMXLI by Amsco Music Publishing Co., Inc., N.Y. City

Made in U. S. A

Stephanie
GAVOTTE

A. CZIBULKA

Copyright MCMXLI by Amsco Music Publishing Co., Inc., N.Y. City

Made in U. S. A.

Minuet l'antique

I. J. PADEREWSKI

Copyright MCMXLI by Amsco Music Publishing Co. Inc., N.Y.City

Made in U.S.A

f Rapidamente melodie

a tempo

Con forza la melodie

cresc.

cresc.

Tales from the Vienna Woods

JOHANN STRAUSS

Copyright MCMXLI by Amsco Music Publishing Co. Inc., N.Y. City

Made in U.S.A.

Passepied

LEO DELIBES

Copyright MCMXLI by Amsco Music Publishing Co. Inc., N.Y. City

Made in U. S. A.

Minuet

L. BOCCHERINI

Copyright MCMXLI by Amsco Music Publishing Co. Inc., N.Y. City

Made in U. S. A.

Anvil Chorus
from "IL TROVATORE"

G. VERDI

Copyright MCMXLI by Amsco Music Publishing Co. Inc., N.Y. City

Made in U. S. A.

Cavatina

JOACHIM RAFF

Larghetto, quasi Andantino

Larghetto, quasi Andantino

Copyright MCMXLI by Amsco Music Publishing Co. N.Y. City

Made in U.S.A.

Caro Nome
from "RIGOLETTO"

GIUSEPPE VERDI

Copyright MCMXLI by Amsco Music Publishing Co. Inc., N.Y. City

Made in U.S.A.

Polonaise
from "MIGNON"

A. THOMAS

Copyright MCMXLI by Amsco Music Publishing Co. Inc., N.Y.City

Made in U.S.A.

Song Without Words

F. MENDELSSOHN, Op. 19, No. 14

Copyright MCMXLI by Amsco Music Publishing Co. Inc., N.Y. City

Eastern Romance

Moderato molto

N. RIMSKY-KORSAKOFF

Moderato molto

Copyright MCMXLI by Amsco Music Publishing Co. Inc., N.Y. City

Made in U. S. A

Sextet
from LUCIA

G. DONIZETTI

Copyright MCMXLI by Amsco Music Publishing Co. Inc., N.Y. City

Made in U.S.A.

Polish Dance

X. SCHARWENKA, Op. 3, No. 1

Copyright MCMXLI by Amsco Music Publishing Co. Inc., N.Y. City

Made in U.S.A.

"Minute" Waltz

FR. CHOPIN, Op. 64, No. 1

Copyright MCMXLI by Amsco Music Publishing Co. Inc., N.Y. City

Made in U.S.A.

Gypsy Rondo

JOSEPH HAYDN

Presto, sempre scherzando

Copyright MCMXLI by Amsco Music Publishing Co. Inc., N.Y. City

Made in U. S. A.

Romance

P. TSCHAIKOWSKY, Op. 5

Copyright MCMXLI by Amsco Music Publishing Co. Inc., N.Y. City

Made in U.S.A.

Pizzicati
SYLVIA BALLET

LEO DELIBES

Allegretto ben moderato

Allegretto ben moderato

Copyright MCMXLI by Amsco Music Publishing Co. Inc., N.Y. City

Made in U. S. A.

102

Rigaudon

JEAN-PHILLIPE RAMEAU

Copyright MCMXLI by Amsco Music Publishing Co. Inc., N.Y. City

Made in U. S. A

Le Secret

L. GAUTIER

Copyright MCMXLI by Amsco Music Publishing Co. Inc., N.Y. City

D.S. 𝄋 al Trio

D.S. 𝄋 al Trio

TRIO

TRIO

Toreador Song

from CARMEN

G. BIZET

Copyright MCMXLI by Amsco Music Publishing Co. Inc., N.Y. City

Made in U. S. A.

Largo

G. F. HÄNDEL

Copyright MCMXLI by Amsco Music Publishing Co. Inc., N. Y. City

Made in U. S. A.

June
(BARCAROLLE)

P. TSCHAIKOWSKY, Op. 37, No. 6

Andante cantabile

Copyright MCMXLI by Amsco Music Publishing Co. Inc., N.Y. City

Made in U.S.A.

Siciliana
from CAVALLERIA RUSTICANA

P. MASCAGNI

Copyright MCMXLI by Amsco Music Publishing Co. Inc., N.Y. City

Made in U.S.A.

Tambourin

JEAN-PHILIPPE RAMEAU.

Copyright MCMXLI by Amsco Music Publishing Co. Inc., N.Y. City

Made in U. S. A.

Spring Dance

EDVARD GRIEG

Copyright MCMXLI by Amsco Music Publishing Co. Inc., N.Y. City

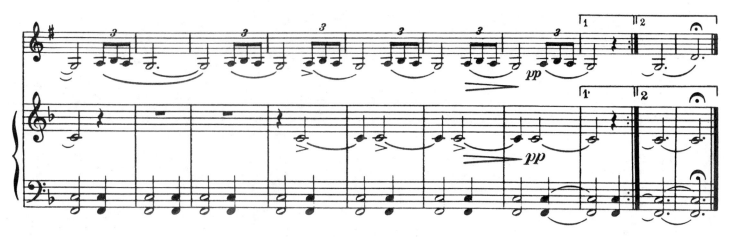

Song of India
from the Legend "SADKO"

N. RIMSKY- KORSAKOFF

Copyright MCMXLI by Amsco Music Publishing Co. Inc., N.Y. City

Made in U.S.A.

Serenade
(LES MILLIONS D'ARLEQUIN)

R. DRIGO

Copyright MCMXLI—by Amsco Music Publishing Co., 240 West 55th St.